Dog's Guide to Helping Others

Published in 2026 by Windmill Books,
an Imprint of Rosen Publishing
2544 Clinton St.
Buffalo, NY 14224

First published in Great Britain in 2022 by Hodder & Stoughton

Credits
Commissioning editor: Sarah Peutrill
Series editor: Lisa Edwards
Series Designer: Rachel Lawston

Cataloging-in-Publication Data
Names: Edwards, Lisa, author. | Roberts, Sian, illustrator.
Title: Dog's guide to helping others / Lisa Edwards, illustrated by Sian Roberts.
Description: Buffalo, NY : Windmill Books, 2026. | Series: Healthy habits
Identifiers: ISBN 9781538399491 (pbk.) | ISBN 9781538399507 (library bound) | ISBN 9781538399514 (ebook)
Subjects: LCSH: Helping behavior--Juvenile literature. | Dogs--Juvenile literature.
Classification: LCC BF637.H4 E393 2026 | DDC 158.3--dc23

Printed in the United States of America

CPSIA Compliance Information: Batch #CSWM26
For Further Information contact Rosen Publishing at 1-800-237-9932

Healthy Habits

Dog's Guide to Helping Others

Lisa Edwards

Siân Roberts

WINDMILL BOOKS

When they are very tiny, puppies like to cuddle their moms.

The puppies feel warm and cared for and Mom feels very happy.

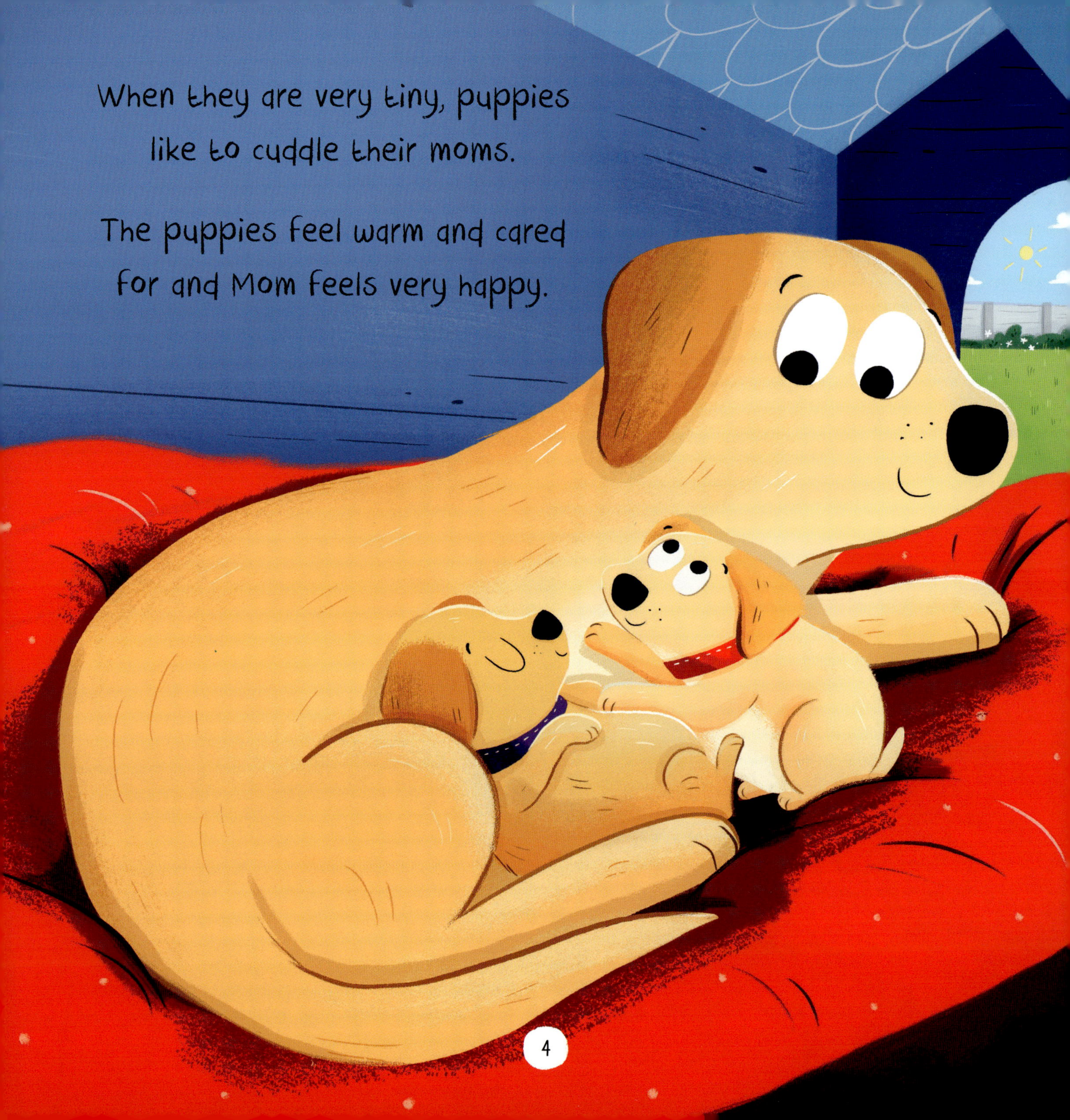

Grandpa loves a hug from his grandpuppies!
We hug people to make them feel loved.

Dogs live in groups called packs.
They share whatever they have between them.

Mom needs to eat enough to make sure she is strong to look after her puppies.

The puppies are very hungry, but they are sharing food.

Sharing things helps others who may not have enough.

It takes puppies around four weeks to learn to walk.
Mom is patient while they try their best.

We can be kind to others who are struggling to learn something, too.

One puppy yaps with delight as her brother walks across the garden for the first time!

Puppies enjoy getting a treat when they learn to do something well.

Grandpa is giving them both a biscuit for walking across the garden!

It is important to thank people who have done something nice for you.

Saying thank you makes you feel good, too.

The puppies are thanking Grandpa by licking his paws!

When they are very young, the puppies need to learn how to share the world.

Mom makes sure that they always behave nicely toward others.

You smile, and say "hello," "please," and "thank you" to be polite to others.

Puppies bark, wag their tails, and lick each other's faces!

Puppies love to play, but one puppy has been playing in the mud!

Mom has to lick her clean.
She doesn't want muddy pawprints everywhere!

We feel happy when we are clean and our beds are tidy.

And so do the puppies!

Dogs love to fetch things
like bones ...
and even bury them for
more fun later!

The puppies are helping Mom by fetching things for her.

You can make other people's lives easier by helping them.

One puppy is so happy to help his mom, he can't stop wagging his tail!

Dogs learn a lot of things from the oldest member of their packs.

Puppies watch and listen carefully to everything they do.

Sometimes people feel lonely and want someone to talk to.
We can help by spending time with them.

Grandpa loves to spend time with his grandpuppies.
They are showing their grandpa how they can walk and run!

Dogs like to play with toys like sticks and balls.
The puppies are play-fighting over the same ball!

In the end, one puppy lets his sister have the ball.

He knows she will feel really happy about it and he can find a new one.

What do you have that you no longer need?

It feels good to receive or give a gift, especially if you've made it yourself.

The puppies are giving their
favorite ball and stick to Mom.

Have you ever made a gift
for someone else?

We enjoy getting together with our friends and family to do something fun.

We like to sing, but dogs like to howl with each other!

The puppies are excited because everyone has joined in!

Everyone feels happy when they do something fun with people they like.

Finally, the puppies are old enough to go outside the garden.

It's time to go to the park!

They like to walk, run, and play games with each other.

What do you like to do in the park?

Isn't it fun when everyone gets together to play?

Taking part in a game or activity helps everyone feel good.

The puppies have learned all about helping others. How can you help?

You can...

Make them feel loved

Share what you have

Be patient and kind

Be polite

Say please and thank you

Be clean and tidy

Help others with chores

Give your time to others

Give away things you no longer need

Make someone a thoughtful gift

Do something fun with friends

Get outdoors with others for exercise

Glossary

Decorate – to add something to an object to make it look nice

Hungry – feeling the need to eat food

Lonely – feeling sad because you have no friends or family around you

Puppy – a young dog

Pack – a group of dogs

Patient – calmly waiting for something to happen

Polite – respectful and kind to others

Struggling – finding something difficult to do

Unexpected – a surprise

Visitor – someone who comes to see you

Let's talk about healthy habits . . .

The *Healthy Habits* series has been written to help young children begin to understand how they can live healthy lives, both in their relationships with others and in their own bodies.

It provides a starting point for parents, caregivers, and teachers to discuss healthy ways of being in the world with little learners. The series involves a cast of animal characters who behave in healthy ways in their own habitats, relating their experiences to familiar, everyday scenarios for children.

Dog's Guide to Helping Others

This story looks at all the ways you can help others, and how it makes *you* feel good, as well as the person (or animal) you are helping.

The book aims to encourage a child's awareness of others, especially when they need help, and to talk about how it feels to help them. It offers children simple tools to use in everyday life, to help those around them.

How to use the book:

The book is designed for adults to share with either an individual child, or a group of children, and as a starting point for discussion.

Choose a time when the children are relaxed and have time to share the story.

Before reading the story:

- Spend time looking at the illustrations and talking about what the book might be about before reading it together. Ask the children to look at the details in each picture to see what all the creatures are doing – some of them are echoing the main themes in the background of the story.
- Encourage children to employ a "phonics-first" approach to tackling new words by sounding them out.

After reading the story:

- Talk about the story with the children. Ask them if they have ever helped another person or animal and how they felt when they did it? What was the recipient's reaction?
- Ask the children why they think it is important to help others and be aware of someone needing help. Does it make them feel good to make someone else's life easier? Does it help them get along with others?
- Place the children into groups. Ask them to think of scenarios when someone might need help and write them down. What could they do to help them?
- At the end of the session, ask one child from each group to read out their scenarios to the others, or even act them out with someone else from the group. Then discuss the different scenarios as a whole class.